KATERI TEKAKWITHA
THE IROQUOIS SAINT

Kateri Tekakwitha
the Iroquois Saint

With an Account of the Iroquois Martyrs
of St. Francis Xavier du Sault

Fr. Pierre Cholonec, S.J.

Translated by
Rev. William Ingraham Kip and
and Ellen H. Walworth

Arx Publishing
Merchantville, NJ

This edition ©2012 by Arx Publishing
Merchantville, New Jersey.

Printed in the United States of America

ISBN 978-1-935228-09-7

Cataloging-in-Publication (CIP) data on file.

PREFACE

St. Kateri Tekakwitha's story means many things to many people—and there are no shortage of biographies of the Lily of the Mohawks. But all of these derivative works must inevitably rely on the primary accounts of her life penned by those who knew her. As important as the primary sources are, however, they are surprisingly not easy to find, so I am pleased to make these available to the public.

Father Pierre Cholonec was one of the two principal biographers of St. Kateri who actually knew her in life. Like his contemporary Fr. Claude Chauchetiere, he wrote a lengthy manuscript biography of her which was only published many years after he died.

Cholonec also sent a letter to his fellow French Jesuits that served as an abridged biography. This letter was first printed in 1715 in an assortment of Jesuit mission texts, and is the first work reproduced in this volume. Though it is an abridgement, it is historically important in that it helped solidify St. Kateri's name and reputation with the Catholic world at large and began the process that would culminate with her canonization nearly 300 years later.

This letter is here followed by one of the most fascinating parts of Cholonec's manuscript biography:

a description of the visions that Father Chauchetiere and Kateri's friend Anastasia had of the saint after death. Her glorious appearance convinced the Jesuit to take to his brushes and create the first icon of this New World saint, a modified version of which is displayed on the front cover. Two prophecies were also made in those visions which later came to pass—one of the church building overturned by a storm, and the other of an Indian being burned at the stake.

In a second letter dated 1715, Father Cholonec left an invaluable account of the martyrs of St. Kateri's mission whose deaths she had foretold. The Iroquois martyrs are unfortunately not very well known, though their stories were passed down for centuries in Canadian literature and appeared in various Indian-language publications in the 1800s. Some of the martyrs' names were also included in a large group of saint's causes that the American bishops forwarded to Rome in the 1940s, but little or nothing seems to have been done to advance their causes since that time.

The two letters of Kateri's life and the Iroquois martyrs are taken from a translation of Cholonec's letters done in the mid-1800s by an Episcopal bishop, Rev. William Ingraham Kip. I have seen fit to emend Kip's translation in spots to bring it in line with contemporary usage. Also, common ethnic and tribal names have been Anglicized, except for a few town names that do not have a ready English equivalent. The translation of the visions comes from an 1891 biography of Kateri by Ellen H. Walworth, again with some minor corrections.

Rejoicing with the Universal Church as the "Genevieve of New France" is raised to the dignity of the altars, it is my prayer that we utilize these precious original sources for spiritual growth and for the development of a richer Katerian iconography. Also, I hope that her canonization inspires greater interest in the causes of her fellow Indians who set such a sterling example of Christian virtue in the mission of St. Francis Xavier, especially those who gave their lives as witnesses for Christ and hallowed our soil with their blood.

—Claudio R. Salvucci, September 2012

CONTENTS

ILLUSTRATIONS

KATERI
TEKAKWITHA,
THE IROQUOIS SAINT

From Father Cholonec, missionary of the Society of Jesus, to Father Augustin Le Blanc of the same Society, procurator of missions in Canada. At Sault de St. Louis, the 27th of August, 1715.

My Reverend Father,

The Peace of our Lord be with you.

The marvels which God is working every day through the intercession of a young Iroquois female who has lived and died among us in the order of sanctity, have induced me to inform you of the particulars of her life, although you have not pressed me in your letters to enter into detail. You have yourself been a witness of these marvels, when you discharged there with so much zeal the duties of a Missionary, and you know that the high Prelate who governs this church, touched by the prodigies with which God has deigned to honor the memory of this holy maiden, has with reason called her the Genevieve of New France. All the French who are in the colonies, as well as the Indians, hold her in singular veneration. They come from a great distance to pray at her tomb, and many, by her intercession, have been immediately cured of their maladies, and have received from Heaven other extraordinary favors. I will write you nothing, my Reverend Father, which I have not myself seen during the time she was under my care, or which I have not learned of the Missionary who conferred on her the rite of holy Baptism.

Tekakwitha (which is the name of this sainted female about whom I am going to inform you) was born in the year 1656, at Caughnawaga, one of the settlements of the lower Iroquois, who are called Mohawks. Her father was an Iroquois and a heathen; her mother, who was a Christian, was an Algonquin, and had been baptized at the village of Three Rivers, where she was brought up among the French. During the time that we were at war with the Iroquois, she was taken prisoner by them, and remained a captive in their country.

We have since learned, that thus in the very bosom of heathenism, she preserved her faith even to her death. By her marriage she had two children, one son and one daughter, the latter of whom is the subject of this narrative, but she had the pain to die without having been able to procure for them the grace of Baptism. The smallpox, which ravaged the Iroquois country, in a few days removed her husband, her son, and herself. Tekakwitha was also attacked like the others, but she did not sink as they did under the violence of the disease. Thus, at the age of four years she found herself an orphan, under the care of her aunts, and in the power of an uncle who was the leading man in the settlement.

The smallpox had injured her eyes, and this infirmity having rendered her incapable of enduring the glare of light, she remained during whole days shut up in her cabin. By degrees she began to love this seclusion, and at length that became her taste, which she had at first endured only from necessity. This inclination for retirement, so contrary to the usual spirit of the young Iroquois, was the principal cause of her preserving her innocence of life while living in such scenes of corruption.

When she was a little older, she occupied herself at home in rendering to her aunts all those services of which she was capable, and which were in accordance with her sex. She ground the corn, went in search of water, and carried the wood; for such, among these Indians, are the ordinary employments of females. The rest of her time she spent in the manufacture of little articles, for which she possessed an extraordinary skill. By this means she avoided two rocks which would have been equally fatal to her innocence—idleness, so common there among her own sex, and which is the source of an infinite number of vices; and the extreme passion they have to spend their time in gossiping visits, and to show themselves in public places where they can display their finery. For it is not necessary to believe that this kind of vanity is confined to civilized nations. The females of our Indians,

Iroquois women at work, from a 1741 engraving.

and especially the young girls, have a great taste for parading their ornaments, some of which they esteem very precious. Their finery consists of cloths which they buy of the Europeans, mantles of fur, and different kinds of shells, with which they cover themselves from head to foot. They have also bracelets, and collars, and pendants for the ears and belts. They adorn even their moccasins, for these personal ornaments constitute all their riches, and it is in this way, by the different kinds of garments, that they mark their rank among themselves.

The young Tekakwitha had naturally a distaste for all this finery which was appropriate to her sex, but she could not oppose the persons who stood to her in the place of father and mother, and to please them she had sometimes recourse to these vain ornaments. But after she became a Christian, she looked back upon it as a great sin, and expiated this compliance of which she had been guilty, by a severe penance and almost continual tears.

M. de Tracy, having been sent by the government to bring to reason the Iroquois nations who laid waste our colonies, carried the war into their country and burned three villages of the Mohawks. This expedition spread terror among the Indians, and they acceded to the terms of peace which were offered them. Their deputies were well received by the French, and a peace concluded to the advantage of both nations.

We availed ourselves of this occasion, which seemed a favorable one, to send missionaries to the Iroquois. They had already gained some smattering of the Gospel, which had been preached to them by Father Jogues, and particularly those of Onondaga, among whom this Father had fixed his residence. It is well known that this Missionary received there that recompense of martyrdom which well befitted his zeal. The Indians at first held him in a severe captivity and mutilated his fingers, and it was only by a kind of miracle that he was able for a time to escape their fury. It seemed however that his blood was destined to be the seed of Christianity in that heathen land, for having had the courage, in the following year, to return for the purpose of continuing his mission among these people who had treated him so inhumanly, he finished his apostolic career amid the torments they forced him to endure. The works of his two companions were crowned by the same kind of death, and it is without doubt to the blood of these first Apostles of the Iroquois nation, that we must ascribe the blessings which God poured out on the zeal of those who succeeded them in this evangelical ministry.

Father Fremin, Father Bruyas, and Father Pierron, who knew the language of the country, were chosen to accompany the Iroquois deputies, and on the part of the French to confirm the peace which had been granted them. They committed also to the Missionaries the presents which the Governor made, that it might facilitate their entrance into these barbarous regions. They happened to arrive there at a time when these people are accustomed to plunge into all kinds of debauchery, and found no one therefore in a fit state to receive them. This unseasonable period however procured for the young Tekakwitha the advantage of knowing early those of whom God wished to make use, to conduct her to the highest degree of perfection. She was charged with the task of lodging the Missionaries, and attending to their wants. The modesty and sweetness with which she acquitted herself of this duty touched her new guests, while she on her part was struck with their affable manners, their regularity in prayer, and the other exercises into which they divided the day. God even then disposed her to the grace of Baptism, which she would have requested if the missionaries had remained longer in her village.

The third day after their arrival they were sent to Tionnontoguen, where their reception was to take place: it was very pompous. Two of the missionaries established themselves in this village, while the third commenced a mission in the village of Oneida which is more than thirty leagues distant in the country.

The next year they formed a third mission at Onondaga. The fourth was established at Seneca and the fifth at the village of Cayuga. The natives of the Mohawk and the Seneca are very numerous, and separated in many different villages, which is the reason why they were obliged to increase the number of the missionaries.

At length Tekakwitha became of a marriageable age, and her relations were anxious to find a husband for her, because, according to the custom of the country, the game which the husband kills in the chase is appropriated to the benefit of his wife and the other members of her family. But the young Iroquois had inclinations very much opposed to the designs of her relations. She had a great love of purity, even before she knew the excellence of this virtue, and anything which could soil it ever so little impressed her with horror. When therefore they proposed to establish her in life, she excused herself under different pretexts, alleging above all her extreme youth, and the little inclination she had to enter into marriage.

The relatives seemed to approve of these reasons; but a little while after they resolved to betroth her when she least expected it, and without even allowing her a choice in the person to whom she was to be united. They therefore cast their eyes upon a young man whose alliance appeared desirable, and made the proposition both to him and to the members of his family. The matter being settled on both sides, the young man in the evening entered the cabin which was destined for him, and seated himself near her. It is thus that marriages are made among the Indians; and although these heathen extend their dissoluteness and licentiousness to the greatest excess, there is yet no nation which in public guards so scrupulously that outward decorum which is the attendant of perfect modesty. A young man would be forever dishonored, if he should stop to converse publicly with a young female. Whenever marriage is in agitation, the business is to be settled by the parents, and the parties most interested are not even permitted to meet. It is sufficient that they are talking of the marriage of a young Indian with a young female, to induce them with care to shun seeing and speaking with each other. When the parents on both sides have agreed, the young man comes by night to the cabin of his future spouse and seats himself near her; which is the same as declaring, that he takes her for his wife, and she takes him for her husband.

Tekakwitha appeared utterly disconcerted when she saw the young man seated by her side. She at first blushed, and then rising abruptly, went forth indignantly from the longhouse; nor would she re-enter until the young man left it. This firmness rendered her relatives outrageous. They considered that they had in this way received an insult, and resolved that they would not be disappointed. They therefore attempted other stratagems, which served only to show more clearly the firmness of their niece.

Artifice not having proved successful, they had recourse to violence. They now treated her as a slave, obliging her to do everything which was most painful and repulsive, and malignantly interpreting all her actions, even when most innocent. They reproached her without ceasing for the want of attachment to her relations, her uncouth manners, and her stupidity, for it was thus that they termed the dislike she felt to marriage. They attributed it to a secret hatred of the Iroquois nation, because she was herself of the Algonquin race. In short, they omitted no means of shaking her constancy.

The young girl suffered all this ill treatment with unwearied patience, and without ever losing anything of her equanimity of mind or her natural sweetness; she rendered them all the services they required with an attention and docility beyond her years and strength. By degrees, her relatives were softened, restored to her their kind feelings, and did not further molest her in regard to the course she had adopted.

At this very time Father Jacques de Lamberville was conducted by Providence to the village of our young Iroquois, and received orders from his superiors to remain there, although it seemed most natural that he should go on to join his brother, who had charge of the mission to the Iroquois of Onnontague.

Tekakwitha did not fail to be present at the instructions and prayers which took place every day in the chapel, but she did not dare to disclose the design she had for a long time formed of becoming a Christian; perhaps, because she was restrained by fear of her uncle, in whose power she entirely was, and who, from interested motives, had joined in the opposition to the Christians; perhaps, because modesty itself rendered her too timid and prevented her from discovering her sentiments to the missionary.

But, at length, the occasion of her declaring her desire for baptism presented itself, when she least expected it. A wound which she had received in the foot detained her in the village, whilst the greater part of the women were in the fields gathering the harvest of Indian corn. The Missionary had selected this time to go his rounds, and instruct at his leisure those who were remaining in the cabins. He entered that of Tekakwitha. This good girl on seeing him was not able to restrain her joy. She at once began to open her heart to him, even in presence of her companions, on the earnest desire she had to be admitted into the fold of the Christians. She disclosed also the obstacles she had been obliged to surmount on the part of her family, and in this first conversation showed a courage above her sex. The goodness of her temper, the vivacity of her spirit, her simplicity and candor, caused the Missionary to believe that one day she would make great progress in virtue. He therefore applied himself particularly to instruct her in the truths of Christianity, but did not think he ought to yield so soon to her entreaties: for the grace of Baptism should not be accorded to adults, and particularly in this country, but with great care and after a long probation. All the winter therefore was employed in her instruction and a rigid investigation of her manner of life.

It is surprising, that notwithstanding the propensity these Indians have for slander, and particularly those of her own sex, the Missionary did not find any one but gave a high encomium to the young catechumen. Even those who had persecuted her most severely were not backward in giving their testimony to her virtue. He therefore did not hesitate any longer to administer to her the holy Baptism which she asked with so much Godly earnestness. She received it on Easter Day in the year 1676, and was named Catherine, and it is thus that I shall call her in the rest of this letter.

The only care of the young neophyte was now to fulfill the engagements she had contracted. She did not wish to restrict herself to the observance of common practices, for she felt that she was called to a more perfect life. Besides the public instructions, at which she was present punctually, she requested also particular ones for the regulation of her private and secret life. Her prayers, her devotions, and her penances were arranged with the utmost exactness, and she was so docile to form herself according to the plan of perfection which had been marked out for her that in a little time she became a model of virtue.

In this manner several months passed away very peaceably. Even her relations did not seem to disapprove of the new course of life which she was leading. But the Holy Spirit has warned us by the mouth of Wisdom, that the faithful soul which begins to unite itself to God, should prepare for temptation; and this was verified in the case of Catherine. Her extraordinary virtue drew upon her the persecutions even of those who admired her. They looked upon a life so pure as being a tacit reproach to their own irregularities, and with the design of discrediting it, they endeavored by divers artifices to throw a taint upon its purity. But the confidence which the neophyte had in God, the distrust she felt of herself, her constancy in prayer, and that delicacy of conscience which made her dread even the shadow of a sin, gave her a perfect victory over the enemies of her innocence.

The exactness with which she observed the festival days at the Chapel was the cause of another storm which came upon her on the part of her relations. The chaplet recited by two choirs is an exercise of these holy days; this kind of psalmody awakens the attention of the neophytes and animates their devotions. They execute the hymns and sacred canticles which our Indians chant, with much exactness and harmony, for they have a fine ear, a good voice, and a rare taste for music. Catherine never omitted this exercise. But they took it ill in the longhouse that on these days she abstained from going to work with the others in the field. At length, they came to bitter words, cast upon her the reproach, that Christianity had made her effeminate and accustomed her to an indolent life; they did not even allow her anything to eat, to oblige her, by means of famine, to follow her relations and to aid in their labor. The neophyte bore with constancy their reproach and contempt, and preferred in those days to do without nourishment rather than violate the law which required the observance of these festivals, or to omit these ordinary practices of piety.

This firmness, which nothing could shake, irritated more and more her heathen relatives. Whenever she went to the Chapel they caused her to be followed with showers of stones by drunken people, or those who feigned to be so, so that, to avoid their insults, she was often obliged to take the most circuitous paths. This extended even to the children, who pointed their fingers at her, cried after her, and in derision called her "the Christian." One day, when she had retired to her cabin, a young man entered abruptly, his eyes sparkling with rage and a hatchet in his hand, which he raised as if to strike her. Perhaps he had no other design than to frighten her. But whatever might have been the Indian's intentions, Catherine contented herself with modestly bowing her head, without showing the least emotion. This intrepidity, so little expected, astonished the Indian to such a degree, that he immediately took to flight, as if he had been himself terrified by some invisible power.

It was in such trials of her patience and piety that Catherine spent the summer and autumn which followed her baptism. The winter brought her a little more tranquiility, but nevertheless, she was not freed from suffering some crosses on the part of one of her aunts. This woman, who was of a deceitful and dangerous spirit, could not endure the regular life of her niece, and therefore constantly condemned her, even in actions and words the most indifferent. It is a custom among these Indians, that uncles give the name of daughters to their nieces, and the nieces reciprocally call their uncles by the name of father. Hence it happens, that first cousins are commonly called brothers. It happened, however, once or twice, that Catherine called the husband of her aunt by his proper name, and not by that of father: but it was entirely owing to mistake or want of thought. Yet this evil spirit did not need any thing farther as the foundation on which to build up a most atrocious calumny. She pretended to believe, that this manner of expressing herself, which seemed to her so familiar, was an evidence of criminal intimacy, and immediately went to seek the missionary, to decry her to him and destroy in his mind those sentiments of esteem which he had always entertained for the neophyte. "Well!" she said, at once, "so Catherine whom you esteem so virtuous, is notwithstanding a hypocrite who deceives you. Even in my presence she solicited my husband to sin." The missionary, who understood the evil spirit of this woman, wished to know on what she founded an accusation of this kind, and having learned what had given occasion to this odious suspicion, he administered to her a severe reprimand, and sent her away utterly confounded. When he afterwards mentioned it to the neophyte, she answered him with a candor and confidence which showed the absence of all falsehood. It was on this occasion that she declared what perhaps we should not have known if she had not been placed on this trial, that by the kindness of the Lord she could not remember that she had ever stained the purity of her person, and that she did not fear receiving any reproach on this point in the day of judgment.

It was sad for Catherine to have to sustain so many conflicts, and to see her innocence exposed without cessation to the outrages and railleries of her countrywomen. And in other respects she had everything to fear in a country where so few of the people had imbibed a taste for the maxims of the Gospel. She, therefore, earnestly desired to be transplanted to some other mission where she might serve God in peace and liberty. This was the subject of her most fervent prayers, and it was also the advice of the missionary, but it was not easy to bring about. She was entirely in the power of an uncle, watchful of all her actions, and through the aversion he had for Christians, incapable of appreciating her resolution. But God who listens favorably even to the simple desires of those who place their trust in Him, disposed all things for the repose and consolation of the neophyte.

A colony of Iroquois had lately been formed among the French, the peace which existed between the two nations having given these Indians an opportunity of coming to hunt on our lands. Many of them stopped near La Prairie de la Madeleine, where the missionaries of our society who dwelt there met them, and at different times conversed with them on the necessity of salvation. God at the same time influencing their hearts by the impressions of his grace, these Indians found themselves suddenly changed, and listened without objection to the proposition that they should renounce their country and settle among us. They received baptism after the usual instructions and probation.

The example and devotion of these new converts drew to them many of their countrymen, and in a few years the Mission of St. Francis Xavier du Sault (for it was thus that it was named) became celebrated for the great number of its neophytes and their extraordinary fervor. If an Iroquois had made these a visit, ever so short, even though he had no other design but to see his relatives or friends, he seemed to lose entirely the desire to return to his own country. The charity of these neophytes led them even to divide with the newcomers the fields which they had cleared with much labor: but the way in which this feeling appeared to the greatest advantage was in the eagerness they showed in instructing them in the truths of our faith. To this work they devoted entire days and even a portion of the night. Their conversations, full of unction and piety, made the most lively impression on the hearts of their guests and transformed them, so to speak, into different beings. He who a little while before breathed of nothing but blood and war, became softened, humble, teachable, and ready to obey the most difficult maxims of our religion.

This zeal did not restrict itself to those who came to visit them, but induced them also to make excursions into the different settlements of their nation, and they always returned accompanied by a large number of their countrymen. On the very day that Catherine received Baptism, one of the most powerful of the Mohawks returned to the mission in company with thirty of the Iroquois of that tribe whom he had gained to Jesus Christ. The neophyte would very willingly have followed him, but she depended, as I have said before, on an uncle who did not see without sorrow the depopulation of his village, and who openly declared himself the enemy of those who thought of going to live among the French.

It was not until the following year that she obtained the facilities she wished for the execution of her design. She had an adopted sister who had retired with her husband to the Mission du Sault. The zeal of the recent converts to draw their relatives and friends to the new colony inspired her with the same thoughts with regard to Catherine, and disclosing her designs to her husband, he gave his consent. He joined himself therefore to an Indian of Lorette and some other neophytes, who under cover of going to trade in beaver skins with the English, travelled to the villages of the Iroquois, with the intention of engaging their acquaintances to follow them and to share in the blessings of their conversion.

With difficulty he reached the village in which Catherine lived and informed her secretly of the object of his journey, and the desire his wife felt that she should be with her at the Mission du Sault, whose praise he set forth in a few words. As the neophyte appeared transported with joy at this disclosure, he warned her to hold herself in readiness to depart immediately on his return from his journey to the English, which he would not have made except to avoid giving umbrage to his uncle. This uncle was then absent, without having any suspicion of his niece's design. Catherine went immediately to take leave of the missionary, and to ask his recommendation to the Fathers who were over the Mission du Sault. The missionary on his part, while he could not withhold his approval of the resolution of the neophyte, exhorted her to place her trust in God, and gave her those counsels which he judged necessary in the present juncture.

As the journey of her brother-in-law was only a pretext the better to conceal his design, he almost immediately returned to the village, and the day after his arrival, departed with Catherine and the Indian of Lorette who had kept him company. It was not long before it was discovered in the village that the neophyte had disappeared, and they had no doubt but that she had followed the two Indians. They immediately therefore despatched a runner to her uncle to give him the news. The old chief, angered at the decrease of his nation, foamed with rage at the intelligence, and immediately charging his gun with three balls, he went in pursuit of those who had accompanied his niece. He made such haste that in a very short time he met up with them.

The two Indians, who had known beforehand that he would not fail to pursue them, had concealed the neophyte in a thick wood and had stopped as if to take a little repose. The old man was very much astonished at not finding his niece with them, and after a moment's conversation, coming to the conclusion that he had credited too easily the first rumor which had been spread, he retraced his footsteps to the village. Catherine regarded this sudden retreat of her uncle as one effect of the protection of God which she enjoyed, and continuing her route she arrived at the Mission du Sault in the end of Autumn of the year 1677.

She took up her abode with the family of her brother-in-law. The cabin belonged to one of the most fervent Christians in the place, named Anastasia, whose care it was to instruct those of her own sex who aspired to the grace of Baptism. The zeal with which she discharged her duty in this employment, her conversations, and her example, charmed Catherine. But what edified her exceedingly was the piety of all the converts who composed this numerous mission. Above all, she was struck with seeing men become so different from what they were when they lived in their own country. She compared their exemplary life with the licentious course they had been accustomed to lead, and recognizing the hand of God in so extraordinary a change, she ceaselessly thanked Him for having conducted her into this land of blessings.

To make a suitable return for these favors from Heaven, she felt that she ought to give herself up entirely to God, without having any reserve, or permitting any thought of herself. The consecrated place became, thenceforth, all her delight. She repaired thither at four o'clock in the morning, attended the Mass at the dawn of day, and afterwards assisted at that of the Indians, which was said at sunrise. During the course of the day she from time to time broke off from her work to go and hold communion with Jesus Christ at the foot of the altar. In the evening she returned again to the church and did not leave it until the night was far advanced. When engaged in her prayers, she seemed entirely unconscious of what was passing without, and in a short time the Holy Spirit raised her to so sublime a devotion, that she often spent many hours in intimate communion with God.

To this inclination for prayer, she joined an almost unceasing application to labor. She sustained herself in her toils by the pious conversations which she held with Anastasia, that fervent Christian of whom I have already spoken, and with whom she had formed a most intimate friendship. The topics on which they most generally talked were the delight they received in the service of God, the means of pleasing him and advancing in virtue, the peculiar traits seen in the lives of the saints, the horror they should have of sin, and the care with which they should expiate by penitence those they had the misfortune to commit. She always ended the week by an exact investigation of her faults and imperfections, that she might efface them by the sacrament of Penance, which she underwent every Saturday evening. For this she prepared herself by different mortifications with which she afflicted her body, and when she accused herself of faults even the most light, it was with such vivid feelings of compunction, that she shed tears and her words were choked by sighs and sobbings. The lofty idea she had of the majesty of God made her regard the least offence with horror, and when any had escaped her, she seemed not able to pardon herself for its commission.

Virtues so marked did not permit me for a very long time to refuse her the permission which she so earnestly desired, that on the approaching festival of Christmas she should receive her first Communion. This is a privilege which is not accorded to those who come to reside among the Iroquois until after some years of probation and many trials; but the piety of Catherine placed her beyond the ordinary rules. She participated, for the first time in her life, in the holy Eucharist, with a degree of fervor proportioned to the reverence she had for this grace and the earnestness with which she had desired to obtain it. And on every subsequent occasion on which she approached the holy Sacrament, it was always with the same disposition. Her manner alone inspired the most lukewarm with devotion, and when a general Communion was about to take place, the most virtuous neophytes endeavored with emulation to be near her, because, said they, the sight alone of Catherine served them for an excellent preparation for communing worthily.

After the festival of Christmas, it being the proper season for the chase, she was not able to excuse herself from following her sister and brother-in-law into the forests. She then made it apparent, that one is able to serve God in all places where his providence calls him. She did not relax any of her ordinary exercises, while her piety even suggested to her holy practices to substitute in place of those which were incompatible with a residence in the forests. There was a time set apart for every thing. In the morning she applied herself to her prayers, and concluded with those which the Indians make in common according to their custom, and in the evening she renewed them again, continuing until the night was far advanced. While the Indians were partaking of their repast to prepare themselves to endure the chase through the whole day, she retired to some secret place to offer up her devotions; as this was a little before the time when they were accustomed to hear Mass at the Mission.

She had fixed a cross in the trunk of a tree which she found by the side of a stream, and this solitary spot was her oratory. There, she placed herself in spirit at the foot of the altar, she united her soul with that of the priest, she prayed her guardian angel to be present for her at that holy sacrifice, and to apply to her its benefits. The rest of the day she spent in laboring with the others of her sex, but to banish all frivolous discourse and preserve her union with God, she always introduced some religious conversation, or perhaps invited them to sing hymns or anthems in praise of their Lord. Her repasts were very simple, and often she did not eat till the end of the day. At other times, she secretly mixed ashes with the food provided for her, to deprive it of everything which might afford pleasure to the taste. This is a self-mortification which she always practised when she could do so without being seen.

This sojourn in the forests was not very agreeable to Catherine, although generally pleasant to the Indian women, because, freed from domestic cares, they pass their time in amusements and feasting. She longed without ceasing for the time to arrive when they are accustomed to return to the village. The Church, the presence of Jesus Christ in the august Sacrament of the Altar, the holy Sacrifice of the Mass, the frequent exhortations, and the other exercises of the Mission of which she was deprived while engaged in the chase—these were the only objects which interested her. She had no taste for anything else. She therefore formed the determination that if she lived to return once more to the Mission, she would never again leave it. She arrived there near the time of Passion Week, and for the first time assisted in the ceremonies of those holy days.

I shall not stop, my Reverend Father, to describe to you here how deeply she was affected by a spectacle so touching as that of the sorrows and death of a God for the safety of men. She shed tears almost continually and formed the resolution to bear for the rest of her days, in her own body, the Cross of Jesus

Christ. From that time she sought all occasions of self-mortification, perhaps to expiate those light faults which she regarded as so many outrages against the Divine Majesty, perhaps to trace in her the image of a God crucified for love of us. The conversations of Anastasia, who often talked with her of the pains of Hell, and the severity which the saints exercised upon themselves, strengthened the desire she had for the austerities of penance. She found herself also animated to this course by an accident which placed her in great danger of losing her life. She was cutting a tree in the woods, which fell sooner than she expected; she had sufficient time, by drawing back, to shun the body of the tree, which would have crushed her by its fall; but she was not able to escape from one of the branches, which struck her violently on the head, and threw her senseless to the ground. She shortly afterwards recovered from her swoon, and those around heard her softly repeating, "I thank thee, good Jesus, for having aided me in this danger." She did not doubt but that God had preserved her to give her time to expiate her sins by repentance. This she declared to a companion who felt herself called, like Catherine, to a life of austerity, and with whom she was in so close an intimacy that they communicated to each other the most secret things which took place in their innermost souls. This new association had indeed so much influence on the life of Catherine that I cannot refrain from speaking of it.

Therese (it is thus that she was named) had been baptized by Father Bruyas in the Iroquois country; but the licentiousness which prevailed among her people and the evil example she always had before her eyes caused her shortly to forget the vows of her Baptism. Even a sojourn which she made after some time at the Mission, where she had come to live with his family, only produced a partial change in her life. A most strange adventure, however, which happened to her, operated at last to her conversion.

She had gone with her husband and a young nephew to the chase, near the river of the Ottawa. On their way some other Indians joined them, and they made a company of eleven persons, that is, four men and four women, with three young persons. Therese was the only Christian. The snow, which this year fell very late, prevented them from having any success in hunting, their provisions were in a short time consumed, and they were reduced to eat some skins, which they had brought with them to make moccasins. At length they ate the moccasins themselves, and finally, pressed by hunger, were obliged to sustain their lives principally by herbs and the bark of trees. In the meantime the husband of Therese fell dangerously ill and the hunters were obliged to halt. Two among them, a Mohawk and a Seneca, asked leave of the party to make an excursion to some distance in search of game, promising to return at the farthest in ten days. The Mohawk, indeed, returned at the time appointed, but he came alone, and reported that the Seneca had perished by famine and misery. They suspected him of having murdered his companion, and then fed upon his flesh; for, although he declared that he had not found any game, he was nevertheless in full strength and health. A few days afterwards the husband of Therese died, experiencing in his last moments deep regret that he had not received Baptism. The remainder of the company then resumed their journey, to attempt to reach the bank of the river and gain the French settlements. After two or three days' march, they became so enfeebled by want of nourishment that they were not able to advance farther. Desperation then inspired them with a strange resolution, which was to put some of their number to death that the lives of the rest might be preserved. They, therefore, selected the wife of the Seneca and her two children, who were thus in succession devoured. This spectacle terrified Therese, for she had good reason to fear the same treatment. Then she reflected on the deplorable state in which conscience told her she was; she repented bitterly that she had ever entered the forest without having first purified herself by a full confession; she asked pardon of God for the disorders of her life and promised to confess as soon as possible and undergo penance. Her prayer was heard, and after incredible fatigues, she reached the village with four others, who alone remained of the company. She did, indeed, fulfill one part of the promise, for she confessed herself soon after her return, but she was more backward to reform her life and subject herself to the rigors of penance.

One day, while she was looking at the new Church they were building at the Sault, after they had removed thither the mission which before had been at La Prairie de la Madeleine, she met with Catherine, who was also inspecting it. They saluted each other for the first time, and entering into conversation, Catherine asked her, which portion of the Church was to be set apart for the females. Therese pointed out the place which she thought would be appropriated to them. "Alas!" answered Catherine, with a sigh, "it is not in this material temple that God most loves to dwell. It is within ourselves that He wishes to take up His abode. Our hearts are the Temple which is most agreeable to Him. But, miserable being that I am, how many times have I forced Him to abandon this heart in which He should reign alone! And do I not deserve, that to punish me for my ingratitude, they should forever exclude me from this temple which they are raising to His glory?"

The humility of these sentiments deeply touched the heart of Therese. At the same time, she felt herself pressed by remorse of conscience to fulfill what she had promised to the Lord, and she did not doubt but that God had directed to her this holy female to support her by her counsels and example in the new kind of life she wished to embrace. She therefore opened her heart to Catherine on the holy desires with which God had inspired her, and insensibly the conversation led them to disclose to each other their most secret thoughts. To converse with greater ease they went and sat at the foot of a cross which was erected on the banks of the St. Lawrence River. This first interview, which

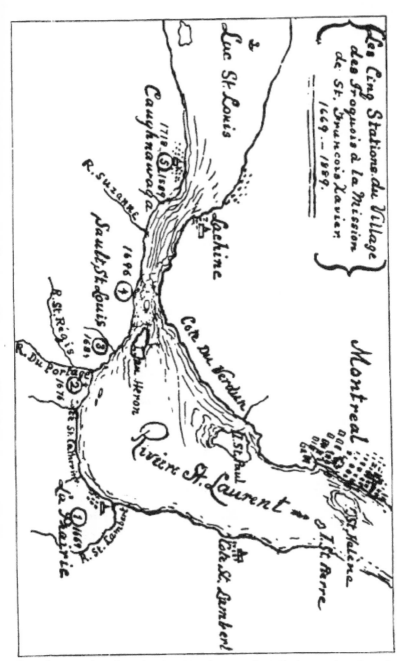

French map showing the five locations of the Mission of St. Francis Xavier. Kateri lived in location #2, to the west of La Prairie.

revealed the uniformity of their sentiments and inclinations, began to strengthen the bonds of a holy friendship which lasted even to the death of Catherine. From this time they were inseparable. They went together to the Church, to the forest, and to their daily labor. They animated each other to the service of God by their religious conversations, they mutually communicated their pains and dislikes, they disclosed their faults, they encouraged each other to the practice of austere virtues, and thus they were mutually of infinite service in advancing more and more in their views of perfection.

It was thus that God prepared Catherine for a new contest which her love of celibacy obliged her to undergo. Interested views inspired her sister with the design of marrying her. She supposed there was not a young man then in the Mission du Sault who would not be ambitious of the honor of being united to so virtuous a female, and that thus having the whole village from which to make her choice, she would be able to select for her brother-in-law some able hunter who would bring abundance to the cabin. She expected indeed to meet with difficulties on the part of Catherine, for she she was not ignorant of the persecutions this generous girl had already suffered, and the constancy with which she had sustained them, but she persuaded herself that the force of reason would finally vanquish her opposition. She selected therefore a particular day, and after having shown Catherine even more affection than ordinary, she addressed her with that eloquence which is natural to these Indians, when they are engaged in anything which concerns their interests.

"I must confess, my dear sister," said she, with a manner full of sweetness and affability, "you are under great obligations to the Lord for having brought you as well as ourselves from our unhappy country, and for having conducted you to the Mission du Sault, where everything is favorable to your piety. If you are rejoiced to be here, I have no less satisfaction at having you with me. You every day indeed increase our pleasure by the wisdom of your conduct, which draws upon you general esteem and approbation. There only remains one thing for you to do to complete our happiness, which is to think seriously of establishing yourself by a good and judicious marriage. All the young girls among us take this course; you are of an age to act as they do, and you are bound to do so even more particularly than others, either to shun the occasions of sin, or to supply the necessities of life. It is true that it is a source of great pleasure to us, both to your brother-in-law and myself, to furnish these things for you, but you know that he is in the decline of life, and that we are charged with the care of a large family. If you were to be deprived of us, to whom could you have recourse? Think of these things, Catherine; provide for yourself a refuge from the evils which accompany poverty; and determine as soon as possible to prepare to avoid them, while you can do it so easily, and in a way so advantageous both to yourself and to our family."

There was nothing which Catherine less

expected than a proposition of this kind, but the kindness and respect she felt for her sister induced her to conceal her pain, and she contented herself with merely answering that she thanked her for this advice, but the step was of great consequence and she would think of it seriously. It was thus that she warded off the first attack. She immediately came to seek me, to complain bitterly of these importunate solicitations of her sister. As I did not appear to accede entirely to her reasoning, and, for the purpose of proving her, dwelt on those considerations which ought to incline her to marriage, "Ah, my father," said she, "I am not any longer my own. I have given myself entirely to Jesus Christ, and it is not possible for me to change masters. The poverty with which I am threatened gives me no uneasiness. So little is requisite to supply the necessities of this wretched life, that my labor can furnish this, and I can always find some miserable rags to cover me." I sent her away, saying, that she should think well on the subject, for it was one which merited the most serious attention.

Scarcely had she returned to the cabin, when her sister, impatient to bring her over to her views, pressed her anew to end her wavering by forming an advantageous settlement. But finding from the reply of Catherine that it was useless to attempt to change her mind, she determined to enlist Anastasia in her interests, since they both regarded her as their mother. In this she was successful. Anastasia was readily induced to believe that Catherine had too hastily formed her resolution, and therefore employed all that influence which age and virtue gave her over the mind of the young girl, to persuade her that marriage was the only part she ought to take.

This measure however, had no greater success than the other, and Anastasia, who had always until that time found so much docility in Catherine, was extremely surprised at the little deference she paid to her counsels. She even bitterly reproached her, and threatened to bring her complaints to me. Catherine anticipated her in this, and after having related the pains they forced her to suffer to induce her to adopt a course so little to her taste, she prayed me to aid her in consummating the sacrifice she wished to make of herself to Jesus Christ and to provide her a refuge from the opposition she had to undergo from Anastasia and her sister. I praised her design, but at the same time advised her to take yet three days to deliberate on an affair of such importance, and during that time to offer up extraordinary prayers that she might be better taught the will of God; after which, if she still persisted in her resolution, I promised her to put an end to the importunities of her relatives. She at first acquiesced in what I proposed, but in less than a quarter of an hour came back to seek me. "It is settled," said she, as she came near me; "it is not a question for deliberation; my part has long since been taken. No, my Father, I can have no other spouse but Jesus Christ." I thought that it would be wrong for me any longer to oppose a resolution which seemed to me inspired by the Holy Spirit, and therefore exhorted her to perseverance, assuring her that I would undertake her defence against those who wished henceforth to disturb her on that subject. This answer restored her former tranquility of mind and reestablished in her soul that inward peace which she preserved even to the end of her life.

Scarcely had she gone when Anastasia came to complain in her turn, that Catherine would not listen to any advice but followed only her own whims. She was running on in this strain, when I interrupted her by saying that I was acquainted with the cause of her dissatisfaction but was astonished that a Christian as old as she was could disapprove of an action which merited the highest praise, and that if she had faith, she ought to know the value of a state so sublime as that of celibacy, which rendered feeble men like to the angels themselves. At these words Anastasia seemed to be in a perfect dream, and as she possessed a deeply seated devotion of spirit, she almost immediately began to turn the blame upon herself; she admired the courage of this virtuous girl, and at length became the foremost to fortify her in the holy resolution she had taken. It was thus that God turned these different contradictions to be a benefit to his servant. And it also furnished Catherine with a new motive to serve God with greater fervor. She therefore added new practices to the ordinary exercises of piety. Feeble as she was, she redoubled her diligence in labor, her watchings, fastings, and other austerities.

It was then the end of Autumn, when the Indians are accustomed to form their parties to go out to hunt during the winter in the forests. The sojourn which Catherine had already made there, and the pain she had suffered at being deprived of the religious privileges she possessed in the village, had induced her to form the resolution, as I have already mentioned, that she would never during her life return there. I thought however that the change of air, and the diet, which is so much better in the forest, would be able to restore her health, which was now very much impaired. It was for this reason that I advised her to follow the family and others who went to the hunting grounds. She answered me in that deeply devotional manner which was so natural to her, "It is true, my Father, that my body is served most luxuriously in the forest, but the soul languishes there, and is not able to satisfy its hunger. On the contrary, in the village the body suffers; I am contented that it should be so, but the soul finds its delight in being near to Jesus Christ. Well then, I will willingly abandon this miserable body to hunger and suffering, provided that my soul may have its ordinary nourishment."

She remained therefore during the winter in the village, where she lived only on Indian corn, and was subjected indeed to much suffering. But not content with allowing her body only this insipid food, which could scarcely sustain it, she subjected it also to austerities and excessive penances, without taking counsel of any one, persuading herself that while the object was self-mortification, she was right in giving herself up to everything which could increase her fervor. She was incited to these holy exercises by the noble examples of self-mortification which she always had before her eyes. The spirit of penance reigned among the Christians at the Sault. Fastings, discipline carried even unto blood, belts lined with points of iron — these were their most common austerities. And some of them, by these voluntary macerations, prepared themselves, when the time came, to suffer the most fearful torments.

The war was once more rekindled between the French and the Iroquois, and the latter invited their countrymen who were at the Mission du Sault to return to their own country, where they promised them entire liberty in the exercise of their religion.

The refusal with which these offers were met transported them with fury, and the Christian Indians who remained at the Sault were immediately declared enemies of their nation. A party of Iroquois surprised some of them while hunting, and carried them away to their country, where they were burned by a slow fire. But these noble and faithful men, even in the midst of the most excruciating torments, preached Jesus Christ to those who were torturing them so cruelly, and conjured them, as soon as possible, to embrace Christianity, to deliver themselves from eternal fires. One in particular among them, named Etienne, signalized his constancy and faith. When environed by the burning flames, he did not cease to encourage his wife, who was suffering the same torture, to invoke with him the holy name of Jesus. Being on the point of expiring, he rallied all his strength, and in imitation of his Master, prayed the Lord with a loud voice for the conversion of those who had treated him with such inhumanity. Many of the Indians, touched by a spectacle so new to them, abandoned their country and came to the Mission du Sault to ask for Baptism and live there in accordance with the laws of the Gospel.

The women were not behind their husbands in the ardor they showed for a life of penance. They even went to such extremes, that when it came to our knowledge, we were obliged to moderate their zeal. Besides the ordinary instruments of mortification which they employed, they had a thousand new inventions to inflict suffering upon themselves. Some placed themselves in the snow when the cold was most severe; others stripped themselves to the waist in retired places, and remained a long time exposed to the rigor of the season, on the banks of a frozen river, and where the wind was blowing with violence. There were even those who, after having broken the ice in the ponds, plunged themselves in up to the neck, and remained there as long as it was necessary for them to recite many times the ten beads of their rosary. One of them did this three nights in succession; and it was the cause of so violent a fever, that it was thought she would have died of it. Another one surprised me extremely by her simplicity. I learned that, not content with having herself used this mortification, she had also plunged her daughter, but three years old, into the frozen river, from which she drew her out half dead. When I sharply reproached her indiscretion, she answered me with a surprising naïveté that she did not think she was doing anything wrong, but that knowing her daughter would one day certainly offend the Lord, she had wished to impose on her in advance the pain which her sin merited.

Although those who inflicted these mortifications on themselves were particular to conceal them from the knowledge of the public, yet Catherine, who had a mind quick and penetrating, did not fail from various appearances to conjecture that which they held so secret, and as she studied every means to testify more and more her love to Jesus Christ, she applied herself to examine everything that was done pleasing to the Lord, that she might herself immediately put it in practice. It was for this reason that while passing some days at Montreal, where for the first time she saw the nuns, she was so charmed with their modesty and devotion that she informed herself most thoroughly with regard to the manner in which these holy sisters lived and the virtues which they practiced. Having learned that they were Christian virgins, who were consecrated to God by a vow of perpetual continence, she gave me no peace until I had granted her permission to make the same sacrifice of herself, not by a simple resolution to guard her virginity, such as she had already made, but by an irrevocable engagement which obliged her to belong to God without any recall. I would not, however, give my consent to this step until I had well proved her and been anew convinced that it was the spirit of God acting in this excellent girl, which had thus inspired her with a design of which there had never been an example among the Indians.

For this great event she chose the day on which we celebrate the Festival of the Annunciation of the most Holy Virgin. The moment after she had received our Lord in Holy Communion, she pronounced with admirable fervor the vow she had made of perpetual virginity. She then addressed the Holy Virgin, for whom she had a most tender devotion, praying her to present to her son the oblation of herself which she had just made; after which she passed some hours at the foot of the altar in holy meditation and in perfect union with God.

From that time Catherine seemed to be entirely divorced from this world, and she aspired continually to Heaven, where she had fixed all her desires. She seemed even to taste in anticipation the sweetness of that heavenly state; but her body was not sufficiently strong to sustain the weight of her austerities and the constant effort of her spirit to maintain itself in the presence of God. She was at length seized with a violent illness, from which she never entirely recovered. There always remained an affliction of the stomach, accompanied by frequent vomiting and a slow fever, which undermined her constitution by degrees, and threw her into a weakness which insensibly wasted her away. It was, however, evident that her soul acquired new strength in proportion as her body decayed. The nearer she approached the termination of her career, the more clearly she shone forth in all those virtues which she had practiced with so much edification. But I need not stop here to particularize them to you, except to mention a few of those which made the most impression and were the source and spring of all the others.

She had a most tender love for God. Her only pleasure seemed to be to keep herself in contemplation in His presence, to meditate on His majesty and mercy, to sing His praises, and continually to desire new ways of pleasing Him. It was principally to prevent distraction from other thoughts that she so often withdrew into solitude. Anastasia and Therese were the only two Christians with whom she wished much to associate, because they talked most of God and their conversations breathed nothing but divine love.

From thence arose the peculiar devotion she had for the Holy Eucharist and the Passion of our Saviour. These two mysteries of the love of the same God, concealed under the veil of the Eucharist and His dying on the cross, ceaselessly occupied her spirit and kindled in her heart the purest flames of love. Every day she was seen to pass whole hours at the foot of the altar, immoveable as if transported beyond herself. Her eyes often explained the sentiments of her breast by the abundance of tears she shed, and in these tears she found

Iroquois village, from a 1741 engraving.

so great delight that she was, as it were, insensible to the most severe cold of winter. Often seeing her benumbed with cold, I sent her to the cabin to warm herself; she obeyed immediately, but the moment after returned to the Church, and continued there in long communion with Jesus Christ.

To keep alive her devotion for the mystery of our Saviour's Passion and to have it always present to her mind, she carried on her breast a little crucifix which I had given her. She often kissed it with feelings of the most tender compassion for the suffering Jesus, and with the most vivid remembrance of the benefits of our redemption. One day wishing particularly to honor Jesus Christ in this double mystery of His love, after having received the Holy Communion, she made a perpetual oblation of her soul to Jesus in the Eucharist and of her body to Jesus attached to the cross; and thenceforth, she was ingenious to imagine every day new ways of afflicting and crucifying her flesh.

During the winter, while she was in the

forest with her companions, she would follow
them at a distance, taking off her shoes and
walking with her naked feet over the ice and
snow. Having heard Anastasia say that of all
torments that of fire was the most frightful,
and that the constancy of the martyrs who
had suffered this torture would be a great
merit with the Lord, the following night
she burned her feet and limbs with a hot
brand, very much in the same way that the
Indians mark their slaves, persuading herself
that by this action she had declared herself
the slave of her Saviour. At another time
she strewed the mat on which she slept with
large thorns, the points of which were very
sharp, and after the example of the holy and
thrice happy Saint Louis de Gonzague, she
rolled herself for three nights in succession
on these thorns, which caused her the most
intense pain. In consequence of these things
her countenance was entirely wasted and pale,
which those around her attributed to illness.
But Therese, the companion whom she had
taken so much into her confidence, having

discovered the reason of this extraordinary paleness, aroused her scruples by declaring that she might offend God if she inflicted such austerities on herself without the permission of her confessor. Catherine, who trembled at the very appearance of sin, came immediately to find me to confess her fault and demand pardon of God. I blamed her indiscretion and directed her to throw the thorns into the fire. She did so immediately, for she had an implicit submission to the judgment of those who directed her conscience, and enlightened as she was by that illumination with which God favored her, she never manifested the least attachment to her own will.

Her patience was the proof of all her acquirements. In the midst of her continual infirmities, she always preserved a peace and serenity of spirit which charmed us. She never forgot herself either to utter a complaint or give the slightest sign of impatience. During the last two months of her life her sufferings were extraordinary. She was obliged to remain night and day in the same position and the least movement caused her the most intense pain. But when these pains were felt with the greatest severity, then she seemed most content, esteeming herself happy, as she herself said, to live and to die on the Cross, uniting her sufferings to those of her Saviour.

As she was full of faith, she had a high idea of everything relating to religion, and this inspired her with a particular respect for those whom God called to the holy ministry. Her hope was firm, her love disinterested, serving God for the sake of God himself, and influenced only by the desire to please Him. Her devotion was tender, even to tears, her communion with God intimate and uninterrupted, never losing sight of Him in all her actions, and it was this which raised her in so short a time to so sublime a state of piety.

In short, there was nothing more remarkable in Catherine than this angelical purity, of which she was so jealous, and which she preserved even to her latest breath. It was indeed a miracle of grace that a young Iroquois should have had so strong an attachment to a virtue so little known in her own country and that she should have lived in such innocence of life during twenty years that she remained in the very midst of licentiousness and dissoluteness. It was this love of purity which produced in her heart so tender an affection for the Queen of Virgins. Catherine could never speak of Our Lady but with transport. She had learned by heart her Litanies and recited them all, particularly in the evening, after the common prayers of the cabin. She always carried with her a rosary, which she recited many times in the course of the day. The Saturdays and other days which are particularly consecrated to her honor, she devoted to extraordinary austerities, and devoted herself to the practical imitation of some of her virtues. She redoubled her fervor when they celebrated one of these Festivals, and she selected such holy days to offer to God some new sacrifice, or to renew those which she had already made.

It was to be expected that so holy a life would be followed by a most happy death.

And so it was in the last moments of her life that she edified us most by the practice of her virtues and above all by her patience and union with God. She found herself very ill towards the time that the men are accustomed to go out to the hunting grounds in the forest, and when the females are occupied from morning even till evening in the fields. Those who are ill are therefore obliged to remain alone through the whole day in their cabins, a plate of Indian corn and a little water having in the morning been placed near their mat. It was in this abandonment that Catherine passed all the time of her last illness. But what would have overwhelmed another person with sadness, contributed rather to increase her joy by furnishing her with something to increase her merit. Accustomed to commune alone with God, she turned this solitude to her profit, and made it serve to attach her more to her Creator by her prayers and fervent meditations.

Nevertheless, the time of her last struggle approached and her strength each day diminished. She failed considerably during the Tuesday of Holy Week, and I therefore thought it well to administer to her Holy Communion, which she recieved with her usual feelings of devotion. I wished also at the same time to give her Extreme Unction, but she told me there was as yet no pressing necessity, and from what she said I thought I would defer it till the next morning. The rest of that day and the following night she passed in fervent communion with our Lord and the Holy Virgin. On Wednesday morning she received Extreme Unction with the same feelings of devotion, and at three hours after mid-day, after having pronounced the holy names of Jesus and Mary, a slight spasm came on, when she entirely lost the power of speech. As she preserved a perfect consciousness even to her last breath, I perceived that she was striving to perform inwardly all the acts which I suggested to her. After a short half hour of agony, she peaceably expired, as if she was only falling into a sweet sleep.

Thus died Catherine Tekakwitha in the twenty-fourth year of her age, having filled the Mission with the odor of her sanctity and the character of holiness which she left behind her. Her countenance, which had been extremely attenuated by the maladies and constant austerities, appeared so changed and pleasant some moments after her death that the Indians who were present were not able to restrain the expression of their astonishment, and declared, that a beam of that glory she had gone to possess was even reflected back on her body. Two Frenchmen who had come from La Prairie de la Madeleine to assist in the services of Thursday morning, seeing her extended on her mat with her countenance so fresh and sweet, said one to the other, "See how peaceably that young female sleeps!" But they were very much surprised when they learned a moment after that it was the body of Catherine who had just expired. They immediately retraced their steps, and casting themselves on their knees at her feet, recommended themselves to her prayers. They even wished to give a public evidence of the veneration they had for the deceased by immediately assisting to make the coffin which was to enclose those holy relics.

I make use of this expression, my Reverend Father, with the greater confidence, because God did not delay to honor the memory of this virtuous girl by an infinite number of miraculous cures, which took place after her death and which still continue to take place daily through her intercession. This is a fact well known not only to the Indians but also to the French at Quebec and Montreal, who often make pilgrimages to her tomb to fulfill their vows or to return thanks for favors which she has obtained for them in Heaven. I could here relate to you a great number of these miraculous cures, which have been attested by individuals the most enlightened and whose probity is above suspicion; but I will content myself with making you acquainted with the testimony of two persons remarkable for virtue and merit, who, having themselves proved the power of this sainted female with God, felt they were bound to leave a public monument for posterity, to satisfy at the same time their piety and their gratitude.

The first testimonial is that of M. de la Colombiere, Canon of the Cathedral of Quebec, Grand-Vicar of the diocese. He expresses himself in these terms:

"Having been ill at Quebec during the past year, from the month of January even to the month of June, of a slow fever, against which all remedies had been tried in vain, and of a diarrhea which even ipecac could not cure, it was thought well that I should record a vow, in case it should please God to relieve me of these two maladies, to make a pilgrimage to the Mission of St. Francis Xavier, to pray at the tomb of Catherine Tekakwitha. On the very same day the fever ceased, and the diarrhea having become better, I embarked some days afterwards to fulfil my vow. Scarcely had I accomplished one third of my journey, when I found myself perfectly cured. As my health is something so very useless that I should not have dared to ask for it, if I had not felt myself obliged to do so by the deference which I ought to have for the servants of the Lord, it is impossible reasonably to withhold the belief that

God, in according to me this grace, had no other view than to make known the credit which this excellent maiden had with Him. For myself I should fear that I was unjustly withholding the truth and refusing to the Missions of Canada the glory which is due to them if I did not testify as I have now done, that I am a debtor for my cure to this Iroquois virgin. It is for this reason that I have given the present attestation with every sentiment of gratitude of which I am capable, to increase, as far as is in my power, the confidence which is felt in my benefactress, but still more to excite the desire to imitate her virtues. Given at Villemarie, the 14th of September, 1696.

J. de la Colombiere, P. J.,
Canon of the Cathedral of Quebec."

The second testimonial is from M. du Luth, Captain in the Marine Corps, and Commander of Fort Frontenac. It is thus that he speaks:

"I, the subscriber, certify to all whom it may concern, that having been tormented by the gout for the space of twenty-three years, and with such severe pains that it gave me no rest for the space of three months at a time, I addressed myself to Catherine Tekakwitha, an Iroquois virgin, deceased at the Sault Saint Louis in the reputation of sanctity, and I promised her to visit her tomb, if God should give me health through her intercession. I have been so perfectly cured, at the end of one novena which I made in her honor, that after five months I have not perceived the slightest touch of my gout. Given at Fort Frontenac, this 15th of August, 1696.

J. DU Luth,
Capt. of the Marine Corps, Commander of Fort Frontenac."

Pierre Cholonec, S.J.

I have thought that a narrative of the virtues of this holy female, born thus in the midst of heathenism and among the Indians, would serve to edify those who having been born in the bosom of Christianity, have also every possible aid in raising themselves to the height of holiness.

I have the honor to be, &c.

VISIONS
OF KATERI
TEKAKWITHA

1680–1682

The sixth day after the death of Catherine, this was Easter Monday, a virtuous person worthy of belief [Father Chauchetiere, —ed] being in prayer at four o'clock in the morning, she appeared to him surrounded with glory, bearing a pot full of maize, her radiant face lifted towards heaven as if in ecstasy. This vision of joy so marvelous was accompanied by three circumstances which rendered it still more admirable. For in the first place it lasted two whole hours, during which this person had leisure to contemplate her at his ease. He did so with a joy and a pleasure that cannot be expressed, Catherine having wished by so signal a favor to acknowledge the great services she had received from him during her life. Furthermore, this same apparition was accompanied with several prophecies by as many symbols which were to be seen on each side of Catherine in her ecstasy; of which prophecies some have been already verified, others have not as yet. For example, at the right appeared a church overturned, and opposite at the left an Indian attached to a stake and burned alive. This vision happened in the month of April of the year 1680.

In 1683, the night of the 20th of August, a storm, so terrible and with so much thunder and lightning that it could only have been caused by the evil spirit, took up the church of the Sault,—60 feet long, of stone masonry,—took it up, I say, at one corner with such violence that, contrary to all likelihood, it turned it over on to the opposite angle and dashed it to pieces. Two of our fathers who were at the church were carried off into the air. A third, who had run to the house to ring the bell, felt the cord suddenly wrenched from his hands, and was carried off like the other two. All three next found themselves on the ground under the debris, from which they were drawn forth with much difficulty; and instead of having their bodies all mangled by so violent a concussion, they came out of it with some slight hurts; this they attributed to the prayers of Catherine, when they all three came together again. As for me, said one, I said Mass today in honor of Catherine. And for me, replied the other, I was this morning at her tomb, to recommend myself to her in a special manner. And as for me, added the third, having for a year past a strong idea that some misfortune was to befall the mission, I have been every day since then, and today again, to pray to Catherine at her tomb to deliver us, and I have not ceased during all that time to importune the superior of the mission to have Catherine's bones transported into our church, without knowing why I did it. Behold what has reference to the overturned church.

As for the Indian seen in this apparition, attached to the stake and burned alive, that was sufficiently verified some years after, when an Indian of this mission was burned at Onondaga, and two women the two following years; and as we do not doubt at all that Catherine, who had made it known so long beforehand, obtained for these Indians the invincible constancy that they showed in their torments, we will speak of it at the end of this third book as a marvelous effect of the power she has in heaven.

Finally, the third circumstance of this apparition, so remarkable, is that in the following year, 1681, on September 1st, and in the year 1682, on April 21st, the same person had the same vision and under the same circumstances; with this only difference, that in the first apparition Catherine was shown to him as a rising sun, with these words which were audible to him: '*Adhuc visio in dies*;' instead of which, in the two following ones, she was shown to him as a sun at midday, with these other words: '*Inspice et fac secundum exemplar*,' God giving him to understand by this, that he wished pictures of Catherine to be painted, which have been worked upon for a long time, and which having been painted, have contributed wonderfully towards making her known; because, having been put on the heads of the sick, they have worked miraculous cures.

Two days after the first of these three apparitions, and eight days after the death of Catherine, she showed herself to her good mother Anastasia in this way. This fervent

Christian, after everybody had gone to bed in her cabin, remained alone in prayer on that evening; and feeling herself finally overcome by sleep she laid down on her mat to rest. But scarcely had she closed her eyes when she was awakened by a voice calling her with these words: 'Mother, arise.' She recognized the voice of Catherine, and at once without the least fear, she raised herself to a sitting posture and turning towards the side from which this voice came, she saw Catherine standing near her all brilliant with light. She had half of her body hidden to the waist in this brightness, and the other half, said this woman, was shining like a sun. She carried in her hand a cross, more brilliant yet than all the rest. So much light came from it that I do not believe one could see anything in the world more beautiful. I saw her, she continued, distinctly in this posture, awake as I was, and she spoke these words to me quite as distinctly: 'Mother, look at this cross; oh! how beautiful it is! It has been my whole happiness during my life, and I advise you also to make it yours.' After these few words she disappeared, leaving her mother full of joy, and her spirit so filled with this vision that after many years she had still the memory of it as fresh as on the first day. It seems that Catherine, in gratitude for the assistance she had received from Anastasia, wished by the sight of that cross so beautiful and so ravishing, and by the words she added, to dispose her to bear generously the one that God was preparing for her; because she has lost since then three of her children killed in war, the eldest of whom was one of the captains of the village; a disaster which she bore with heroic constancy, so much had she been fortified within by this apparition of her dear daughter.

Catherine was seen also by her companion, one day when she was alone in her cabin. She sat down beside her on her mat, recalled to her something she had done, and after giving her some advice for her conduct, she withdrew. As for the rest, the great affection Catherine had for the cross, and the manner in which she appeared to her mother Anastasia, gave the idea of painting her with the cross in her hand as the posture most suitable to her.

But God has spoken still more clearly as to the sanctity and merit of Catherine, His spouse, by authentic testimony. I mean those prodigious graces, and so numerous, that He has already bestowed and continues to bestow through her intercession, on every sort of people.

THE
IROQUOIS
MARTYRS

1688–1693

From Father Cholonec, missionary of the Society of Jesus in New France, to Father Jean-Baptiste de la Halde of the same Society.

My Reverend Father,

The Peace of our Lord be with you.

I have learned with much consolation that you have been edified in France by the account which I sent of the virtues of a young Iroquois virgin, who died here in the odor of sanctity, and whom we regard as the Protectress of this colony. It is the mission of St. Francis Xavier du Sault which trained her to Christianity, and the impressions which such examples have left there still remain, and will remain for a long time, as we hope, through the mercy of God. Long before it occurred, she had predicted the glorious death of some Christians of this Mission, and we have reason to believe that she is the one who, from the Heaven where she is placed, has sustained the courage of these generous devoted men, who have signalized their constancy and faith in the midst of the most frightful sufferings. I will relate to you, therefore, in a few words, the history of these fervent neophytes, for I am persuaded that you will be touched by it.

ETIENNE TE GANONAKOA

The settlements of the Iroquois had been gradually depopulated by the desertion of many families, who took refuge in the Mission du Sault for the purpose of embracing Christianity there. Etienne te Ganonakoa was of this number. He came to reside there with his wife, a sister-in-law, and six children. He was then about thirty-five years of age; his natural disposition had nothing in it that was barbarous, and the stability of his marriage in a country where the most perfect license reigns, and where they easily change their wives, was one evidence of the innocency of the life which he had led. All the newcomers urgently desired Baptism, and it was granted them after the customary probation and instructions.

We were immediately edified in the village by the union which evidently existed in this family, and the care with which they honored God. Etienne watched the education of his children with a zeal worthy of a missionary. Every day, both morning and evening, he sent them to prayers, and to the instructions which are provided for those of that age. Nor did he fail himself to set them an example, by the constancy of his attendance at all the exercises of the Mission, and by his frequent participation in the Sacraments.

It was by such a course of Christian conduct that he prepared himself to triumph over the enemies of religion, and to defend his faith in the midst of the most cruel torments. The Iroquois had used every means to induce those of their countrymen who were at the Sault to return to their native land. But their prayers and presents having been found useless, they resorted to menaces, and signified to them, that if they persisted in their refusal, they should no longer regard them as relatives or friends, but their hate would become irreconcilable, and they would treat them as declared enemies. The war which was then existing between the French and Iroquois furnished them with a pretext for spending their rage on those of their countrymen who, after having thus deserted them, fell into their hands. It was at this time, in the month of August, 1690, that Etienne set out for the purpose of hunting, in the autumn, accompanied by his wife and another Indian of the Sault. In the following month of September, these three neophytes were surprised in the woods by a party of the enemy, consisting of fourteen Cayugas who seized them, bound them, and carried them away prisoners into their country.

As soon as Etienne saw himself at the mercy of the Cayugas he did not for a moment doubt but that he would shortly be delivered up to a most cruel death. He expressed himself thus to his wife, and recommended to her, above all things, to remain steadfast to her faith, and in case she should ever be permitted to return to the Sault, to bring up her children in the fear of God. During the whole journey he did not cease exhorting her to constancy and endeavoring to fortify her against the dangers to which she was about to be exposed among those of her own nation.

The three captives were conducted not to Cayuga where it was most natural that they should carry them, but to Onondaga. God determined, it seemed, that the steadfastness and constancy of Etienne should shine forth in a place which was at that time celebrated for the crowds of Indians who were assembled about it, and who, while there, plunged themselves in the most infamous debaucheries. Although it is their custom to await the arrival of their captives at the entrance of the village, yet the joy they felt at having some of the inhabitants of the Sault in their power induced them to go forth a great distance from their setttlement to meet their prey. They had arrayed themselves in their finest dresses as for a day of triumph—they were armed with knives and hatchets and clubs, and anything on which they could lay their hands, while fury was painted on their countenances. As soon as they joined the captives, one of the Indians came up to Etienne.

"My brother," said he, "your end has come. It is not we who put you to death, but you sealed your own fate when you left us to live among the Christian dogs."

"It is true," answered Etienne, "that I am a Christian, but it is no less true that I glory in being one. Inflict on me what you please, for I fear neither your outrages nor torments. I willingly give up my life for that God who has shed all his blood for me."

Scarcely had he uttered these words, when they furiously threw themselves upon him, and cut him cruelly on his arms, his thighs, and over his whole body, which in an instant they covered with blood. They cut off several of his fingers, and tore out his nails. Then, one of the troop cried out to him, "Pray to God."

"Yes, I will pray to Him," said Etienne; and raising his bound hands, he made as far as he was able the sign of the cross, at the same time pronouncing with a loud voice, in their language, these words, "In the name of the Father," &c.

Immediately they cut off half his fingers which remained, and cried to him a second time, "pray to God now."

Etienne made anew the sign of the cross, and the instant that he did so, they cut off all his fingers down to the palm of his hand.

Then a third time they invited him to pray to God, insulting him, and pouring out against him all the injuries which their rage could dictate. As this generous neophyte commenced the attempt to make the sign of the cross with the palm of his hand, they cut it off entirely. Not content with these first sallies of fury, they gashed his flesh on all the places which he had marked with the sign of the cross, that is to say, on his forehead, on his stomach, and from one shoulder to the other, as if to efface those august marks of religion, which he had impressed there.

After this bloody prelude, they conducted the prisoners to the village. They at first bound Etienne before a large fire which they had kindled there, and in which they had heated some stones red hot. These stones they placed between his thighs and pressed them violently against each other. They then ordered him to chant after the Iroquois manner, and when he refused to do so, and, on the contrary, repeated in a loud voice the prayers he was accustomed to recite every day, one of the furious Indians about him seized a burning brand, and struck him forcibly on the mouth; then, without giving him time to breathe, they bound him to the stake.

When the neophyte found himself in the midst of the red-hot irons and burning brands, far from showing any fear, he cast a tranquil look upon all the ferocious brutes who surrounded him, and spoke to them thus: "Satisfy yourselves, my brethren, with the barbarous pleasure you experience in burning me; do not spare me, for my sins merit much more of suffering than you can procure me; the more you torment me, the more you augment the recompense which is prepared for me in Heaven."

These words served only to enflame their fury. The inhabitants all with a kind of emulation seized the burning brands and red-hot irons, with which they slowly burned all the body of Etienne. The courageous neophyte suffered all these torments without allowing a single sigh to escape him. He seemed to be perfectly tranquil, his eyes being raised to heaven, whither his soul was drawn in continual prayer. At length, when he perceived his strength failing, he requested a cessation for a few moments, and then reviving all his fervor, he uttered his last prayer. He commended his soul to Jesus Christ, and prayed him to pardon his death to those who had treated him with so much inhumanity. At last, after new torments suffered with the same constancy, he gave up his soul to his Creator, triumphing, by his courage, over all the cruelty of the Iroquois.

They granted her life to his wife, as he had predicted to her. She remained sometime longer a prisoner in their country, but without either entreaties or threats being able to vanquish her faith. Having returned to the Mohawk village, which was her native place, she remained there until her son came to seek her and conducted her back to the Sault.

With regard to the Indian who was taken at the same time with Etienne, he escaped with the loss of some of his fingers which were cut off and a deep cut which he received on his leg. He was carried afterwards to Cayuga, where they granted him his life. They used every effort to induce him to marry there and live in the customary debauchery of the nation; but he answered constantly, that his religion forbade him to indulge in these excesses. At last, having gone towards Montreal with a party of warriors, he secretly withdrew from his companions, and returned to the Mission du Sault, where he has lived since with much piety.

Françoise Gonannhatenha

Two years afterwards, a female of the same Mission gave an example of constancy equal to that of Etienne and finished her life, as he did, in the flames. She was named Françoise Gonannhatenha. She was from Onondaga and had been baptized by the Father Fremin. All the Mission was edified by her piety, her modesty, and the charity she exercised towards the poor. As she herself had abundance, she divided her goods among many families, who were thus sustained by her liberality. Having lost her first husband, she married a virtuous Christian who as well as herself was from Onondaga and who had lived a long time at Chasteau-Guay, which is three leagues distant from the Sault. He passed all his summers there in fishing and happened to be actually there when news was received of an incursion of the enemy. Immediately Françoise placed herself in a canoe with two of her friends, to go in search of her husband, and deliver him from the peril in which he was involved. They arrived there in time, and the little party thought itself in security, when at the distance of only a quarter of a league from the Sault, they were unexpectedly surprised by armed enemies who were composed of Onondagas, Senecas, and Cayugas. They immediately cut off her husband's head, and the three women were carried away prisoners.

The cruelty which was exercised towards them the first night which they passed in the Iroquois camp, led them to realize that the most inhuman treatment awaited them. The inhabitants diverted themselves with tearing out their nails and burning their fingers in their pipes, which is, they say, a most dreadful torture.

Their runners carried to Onondaga the news of the prize which they had taken, and the two friends of Françoise were immediately given to Oneida and to the Seneca while Françoise herself was surrendered to her own sister, who was a person of great consideration in the village. But she, putting aside the tenderness which her nature and blood should have inspired her, abandoned her to the discretion of the old men and warriors, that is to say, she destined her to the fire.

No sooner had the prisoners arrived at Onondaga than they forced Françoise to ascend a scaffolding which was erected in the middle of the village. There, in the presence of her relatives and all her nation, she declared with a loud voice that she was a Christian of the Mission du Sault, and that she thought herself happy to die in her country and by the hands of her kinsmen, after the example of Jesus Christ, who had been placed on the cross by the members of His own nation, whom he had loaded with benefits.

One of the relatives of the neophyte who was present had made a journey to the Sault five years before for the purpose of inducing her to return with him. But all the artifices which he employed to persuade her to abandon the Mission were useless. She constantly answered him that she prized her faith more than she did either country or life, and that she was not willing to risk so precious a treasure. The Indian had for a long time nourished in his heart the indignation which he had conceived on account of this resistance and now, being again still more irrritated by listening to the speeches of Françoise, he sprang on the scaffolding, snatched from her a crucifix which hung from her neck, and with a knife which he held in his hand, made on her breast a double gash in the form of a cross. "Hold," said he, "see the cross which you esteem so much, and which prevented you from leaving the Sault when I took the trouble to go and seek you."

"I thank you, my brother," Françoise answered him. "It was possible to lose the cross which you have taken from me, but you have given me one which I can lose only with my life."

She continued afterwards to address her countrymen on the mysteries of her faith, and she spoke with a force and unction which were far beyond her ability and talents. "In conclusion," said she, "however frightful may be the torments to which you destine me, do not think that my lot will be to complain. Tears and groans rather become you. This fire which you kindle for my punishment will only last a few hours, but for you a fire which will never be extinguished is prepared in hell. Nevertheless, you still have the opportunity to escape it. Follow my example, become Christians, live according to the rules of this so holy law, and you will avoid these eternal flames. Still, however, I declare to you that I do not wish any evil to those whom I see preparing everything to take away my life. Not only do I pardon them for my death, but I again pray the Sovereign Arbiter of life and death to open their eyes to the truth, to touch their hearts, to give them grace to be converted and to die Christians like myself."

These words of Françoise, far from softening their hearts, only increased their fury. For three nights in succession they led her about through all the longhouses to make sport for the brutal populace. On the fourth they bound her to the stake to burn her. These furies applied to her, in all parts of her body, burning brands, and gun barrels red hot. This suffering lasted many hours, without this holy victim giving utterance to the least cry. She had her eyes ceaselessly elevated to Heaven, and one would have said that she was insensible to these excruciating pains. M. de Saint Michel, Seigneur of the place of that name, who was then a prisoner at Onondaga and who escaped as if by miracle from the hands of the Iroquois, only one hour before he was to have been burned, related to us all these circumstances of which he was a witness. Curiosity attracted around him all the inhabitants of Montreal, and the simple account of what he had seen drew tears from every one. They were never tired of hearing him speak of a courage which seemed so wonderful.

When the Iroquois have amused themselves a sufficient length of time with burning their prisoners by a slow process, they cut them round the head, take off their scalp, cover the crown of the head with hot ashes, and take them down from the stake. After which they take a new pleasure in making them seen, pursuing them with terrific shouts, and beating them unmercifully with stones. They adopted this plan with Françoise.

M. de Saint-Michel says that the spectacle made him shudder; but a moment afterwards he was excited even to tears when he saw this virtuous neophyte throw herself on her knees, and raising her eyes to heaven offer to God in sacrifice the last breath of life which remained. She was immediately overwhelmed with a shower of stones which the Iroquois cast at her and died, as she had lived, in the exercise of prayer and in union with our Lord.

MARGUERITE GARONGOUAS

In the following year a third victim of the Mission du Sault was sacrificed to the fury of the Iroquois. Her sex, her extreme youth, and the excess of torment which they caused her to suffer rendered her constancy most memorable. She was named Marguerite Garongouas, twenty-four years of age, a native of Onondaga, and she had received Baptism at the age of thirteen. She was married shortly afterwards, and God blessed her marriage in giving her four children whom she brought up with great care in the precepts of religion. The youngest was yet at the breast, and she was carrying it in her arms at the time of her capture.

It was in the Autumn of the year 1693, that having gone to visit her field at a quarter of a league from the fort, she fell into the hands of two Onondagas who were from her own country, and it is even probable that they were her relatives. The joy which had been felt at Onondaga at the capture of the first two Christians of the Sault, led these Indians to believe that this new capture would win for them the greatest applause. They therefore carried her with all speed to the town.

At the first news of her arrival, all the Indians poured out of the village and went to await the prisoner on an eminence which it was necessary for her to pass. A new fury seemed to possess their minds. As soon as Marguerite came in sight, she was received with frightful cries, and when she reached the eminence, she saw herself surrounded by all the Indians, to the number of more than four hundred. They first snatched her infant from her, then tore off her clothes, and at last cast themselves upon her pell-mell, and began cutting her with their knives, until her whole body seemed to be but one wound. One of our Frenchmen who was a witness of this terrible spectacle, attributed it to a kind of miracle that she did not expire on the spot. Marguerite saw him, and calling him by name, exclaimed, "Alas! You see my destiny, that only a few moments more of life remain to me. God be thanked, however, I do not at all shrink from death, however cruel may be the form in which it awaits me. My sins merit even greater pains. Pray the Lord that He will pardon them to me, and give me strength to suffer."

She spoke this with a loud voice, and in their language. One cannot be sufficiently astonished, that in the sad state to which she was reduced, she had so much spirit remaining.

After a little while they conducted her to the cabin of a French woman, an inhabitant of Montreal, who was also a prisoner. She availed herself of the opportunity to encourage Marguerite and to exhort her to suffer with constancy these short-lived pains in view of the eternal recompense by which they would be followed. Marguerite thanked her for her charitable counsels and repeated to her what she had already said, that she had no fears of death but would meet it with good courage. She added also, that since her Baptism she had prayed to God for grace to suffer for his love, and that seeing her body so mangled, she could not doubt but that God had favorably heard her prayer. She was therefore contented to die, and wished no evil to her relatives or countrymen who were about to be her executioners, but on the contrary, she prayed God to pardon their crime and give them grace to be converted to the faith. It is indeed a remarkable fact, that the three neophytes of whom I have spoken, all prayed in the hour of death for the salvation of those who were treating them so cruelly; and this is a most tangible proof of the spirit of charity which reigned at the Mission du Sault.

These two captives were conversing on eternal truths and the happiness of the saints in Heaven, when a party of twenty Indians came to seek Marguerite, to conduct her to the place where she was to be burned. They paid no regard to her youth, nor her sex, nor her country, nor the advantage she possessed in being the daughter of one of the most distinguished men of the village, one who held the rank of chief among them, and in whose name all the affairs of the nation were carried on. These things would certainly have saved the life of any one else but a Christian of the Mission du Sault.

Marguerite was then bound to the stake, where they burned her over her whole body with a cruelty which it is not easy to describe. She suffered this long and severe torture without showing the least sign of sorrow. They only heard her invoke the holy names of Jesus, of Mary, and of Joseph and pray them to sustain her in this rude conflict, even until her sacrifice was completed. From time to time she asked for a little water, but after some reflection, she prayed them to refuse it to her, even when she might ask for it.

"My Saviour," said she, "was thirsty while dying for me upon the Cross. Is it not right therefore, that I should suffer the same inconvenience?" The Iroquois tormented her from noon even to sunset. In the impatience they felt to see her draw her last breath, before the night should oblige them to retire, they unbound her from the stake, took off her scalp, covered her head with the hot cinders, and ordered her to run. She on the contrary, threw herself on her knees, and raising her eyes and hands to Heaven, commended her soul to the Lord. The barbarians then struck her on the head many blows of a club without her discontinuing her prayer, until at last one of them, crying out, "Is it not possible for this Christian dog to die?" took a new knife and thrust it into the lower part of her stomach. The knife, although struck forward with great swiftness, snapped off to the entire astonishment of the inhabitants, and the pieces fell at her feet. Another then took the stake itself to which she had been bound, and struck her violently on the head. As she still gave some signs of life, they heaped on the fire a pile of dry wood which happened to be in that place, and then cast her body on it, where it was shortly consumed. It is from thence that Marguerite went without doubt to receive in Heaven the recompense which was merited by a sainted life terminated by so precious a death.

It was natural that they should grant its life to her child. But an Iroquois to whom it had been given wished to avenge himself on it for an affront which he thought he had received from the French. Three days after the death of Marguerite they were surprised at hearing, at the beginning of the night, the cry of death. At this cry, all the inhabitants sallied forth from their cabins to repair to the place from which it proceeded. The inhabitant of Montreal, of whom I have spoken, ran thither with the rest. There they found a fire burning and the infant ready to be cast into it. The inhabitants could not help being softened at this spectacle; but this was still more the case, when the infant, who was but a year old, raising its little hands to heaven, with a sweet smile, called three times on its mother, showing by its gesture that it wished to embrace her. The inhabitant of Montreal did not doubt but that its mother had appeared to it.

It is at least probable that she had asked from God that her child should be reunited to her before long, that it might be preserved from the licentious training it would have, which would withdraw it as far as possible from Christianity. Although, as it happened, the infant was not abandoned to the flames, for one of the most considerable men of the village delivered it from them; yet it was only to devote it to a death scarcely less cruel. He took it by the feet, and raising it in the air, dashed its head against a stone.

ETIENNE HAONHOUENTSIONTAOUET

I cannot forbear, my Reverend Father, speaking to you once more of a fourth neophyte of this Mission, who, although he escaped the fire which was prepared for him, nevertheless had the happiness of giving his life rather than be exposed to the danger of losing his faith. It was a young Mohawk, named Haonhouentsiontaouet. He was captured by a party of the Mohawks, who carried him away as a slave into their own country. As he had many relations, they granted him his life, and gave him to those who belonged to the same family. These were urgent in their solicitations that he should live according to the customs of the nation; that is to say, indulge in all the disorders of a licentious life. Etienne, far from listening to them, gave in reply the truths of salvation, which he explained with much force and unction, and ceaselessly exhorted them to go with him to the Mission du Sault, there to embrace Christianity. But he spoke to people born and educated in vice, the habit of which was too sweet to enable them to quit it. Thus, the example and the exhortations of the neophyte served no other purpose than to render them more guilty in the sight of God.

As it seemed that his residence at the Mohawk town was of no advantage to his relatives, and that it might be even dangerous to his own salvation, he adopted the resolution to return to the Sault. He disclosed his intention to those around him, and they consented to it the more willingly, because they saw that they would thus be delivered from an importunate censor, who was continually condemning the vices of the nation. He therefore a second time quitted his country and his family, for the sake of preserving that faith which was more dear to him than everything else.

Scarcely, however, had he set out on his journey, when the report of his departure spread through the longhouses. It was particularly mentioned in one, in which some intoxicated young men were at that time actually engaged in a debauch. They were enraged against Etienne, and after pouring out their abuse against him, concluded that it would not do to suffer him thus to prefer the Christian settlement to his own country, that this was an affront which reflected on the whole nation, and that they were bound to constrain the Christian dog to return to the village, or cut off his head, for the purpose of intimidating those who might be tempted to follow his example.

Three of them, therefore, immediately armed themselves with hatchets and ran after Etienne. They shortly met up with him and, holding a hatchet raised over his head, said roughly, "Retrace your steps and follow us. It will be your death to resist, for we have orders from the Sachems to cut off your head." Etienne answered them with his usual sweetness, that they were masters of his life, but that he preferred losing that to risking his faith and salvation in their village; that he was, therefore, going to the Mission du Sault, where he was resolved to live and die.

As he saw that after this particular declaration of his sentiments, these brutes would undoubtedly destroy him, he requested them to give him a few moments in which to pray to God. They had this condescension, intoxicated as they were, and Etienne threw himself on his knees, and tranquilly offered up his prayer, in which he thanked God for the grace which had been given him to die a Christian. He prayed, too, for his heathen relatives and in particular for his murderers, who, at that very moment raised their hatchets and split open his head.

We were informed of the particulars of this death, so noble and Christian, by some Mohawks who came shortly after to fix their residence at the Mission du Sault.

Jeanne Gouastahra

I will finish this letter by the history of another Christian of this Mission, whose life has been a model of patience and piety. It was the earliest companion of Catherine Tekakwitha and the most faithful imitator of her virtues. Jeanne Gouastahra, for such was her name, was of the nation of the Oneida. She was married to a young Mohawk at the Mission of Notre-Dame de Lorette, and her natural sweetness of character and rare virtue ought to have attracted to her all the tenderness of her husband. But the young man abandoned himself to the customary vices of his nation, that is to say, to intemperance and licentiousness, and his dissoluteness was to the neophyte a constant source of bad treatment. He sometime afterwards left the village of Lorette, and became a wanderer and a vagabond. His virtuous wife, however, was not willing to leave him. She followed him wherever he went, in the hope of at last inducing him to return to himself and thus gaining him to Jesus Christ; she endured his debaucheries and brutalities with unalterable patience; she even practised frequent austerities in secret to obtain his conversion from God. The unhappy man took it into his head to come to the Sault, where he had relatives, and she accompanied him thither, and exhibited towards him those attentions and acts of kindness which should have been able to soften the hardest heart. At last, after many changes, having plunged deeply into licentiousness and dissoluteness, he entirely renounced his faith, and returned to the Mohawks. This was the only place to which the neophyte refused to follow him. She had, however, the prudence to go and live at Lorette, with the relatives of her unworthy husband, hoping that this last proof of complaisance would induce him to abandon his debaucheries. But she had not passed a year there, when she learned that this apostate had been killed by some Indians, whose longhouse he had attacked when he had gone out after a debauch which had been extended to the last excess.

A death so bad touched her deeply. Although she was still in the flower of her age, she forever renounced all thoughts of the marriage state, and determined to pass the rest of her days near the tomb of Catherine. There she lived as a Christian widow, striving to sanctify herself by the practice of all virtues, and by continual austerities. And there she shortly afterwards died, in the odor of sanctity. One thing only gave her pain in her last illness. She was leaving behind her two children, still in their tender age, the one not having yet reached its sixth year, nor the other its fourth, and she feared lest, in process of time, they should be corrupted and follow in the steps of their unhappy father. She had, therefore, recourse to our Lord with that fervor and confidence which animated all her prayers, and she asked of Him the favor that the children should not be separated from their mother. Her prayer was favorably heard, and although the two children were then in perfect health, the one became ill immediately and died before the mother, while the other followed eight days after her own departure.

I should continue indefinitely, my Reverend Father, if I were to speak again of many other neophytes whose virtue and faith were equally tried. What, however, I have already written will suffice to give some idea of the fervor which reigns in the Mission of St. Francis Xavier du Sault. His Grace the Bishop of Quebec, who visited our neophytes, has given his public testimony to their virtue. It is thus that this high Prelate speaks in a relation which he gave of the state of New France, and which was published in 1688: "The ordinary life of all these Christians has nothing about it which is common, and one might take it for a veritable monastery. As they have abandoned all the advantages of their own country, for the sole reason that they might secure their salvation near the French, we can there see everything arranged for the practice of the most perfect freedom from worldly passions, and they preserve among themselves so admirable a method to promote their holiness, that it would be difficult to add anything else."

I hope, my Reverend Father, that your zeal will often lead you to pray to the God of mercy for these new converts, to the end that He would preserve them in that state of fervor in which He has placed them by His grace. With every sentiment of respect.

+

RELATED TITLES

The Annual Narrative of the Mission of the Sault From Its Foundation Until the Year 1686
by Claude Chauchetiere, S.J.

Chauchetiere was a French Jesuit who penned this fascinating year-by-year chronicle of the famous Native American mission which drew converts from over 20 tribes and was the home of St. Kateri Tekakwitha. Drawing from the writings of his fellow missionaries as well as his own personal knowledge, Chauchetiere begins with the mission's founding at La Prairie in 1667 by Catherine Gandeaktena, an Erie convert known as the Mother of the Poor.

As Christian Iroquois fled persecution in their homeland, the mission swelled to become "the asylum of those who wished sincerely to pray to God". Yet even with "the forces of hell unchained against the mission" — unscrupulous liquor dealers, dissolute women, hostile French governors and Iroquois pagans—the Sault's Christian faith remained unshaken, and it survived to become the nucleus of an authentically Native Church throughout Canada and the northern United States.

2006 • 70pp • paperback • 1-889758-75-2 • $18.95

The Roman Rite in the Algonquian and Iroquoian Missions From the Colonial Period to the Second Vatican Council
by Claudio R. Salvucci

Representing the first general treatment of the "Indian Mass" of the North American Catholic missions, this volume draws on historical descriptions as well as rare missionary manuscripts and publications to trace the development of the distinctive American Indian liturgies from the early hymn singing of the mid-1600s to the adaptation of vernacular plainchant and polyphony. Weaving together extensive primary source quotations, Salvucci overturns popular misconceptions of missionaries as cultural imperialists, showing instead how native congregations and scholarly priests worked together in adapting the rich traditions of Counter-Reformation Roman Catholicism to the linguistic and cultural needs of the New World.

This volume further compares and contrasts the Indian Masses of different missions with each other and with the official Roman Missal. It also contains chapters on the calendar and hagiography of the missions; formulas for Baptism, Matrimony, and other sacraments; the Divine Office; characteristic sacramentals and devotions; and religious life. Extensive appendices are included, such as the entire text of a Mohawk Indian Mass; propers and ordinaries for other missions including those of the Algonquins, Abenaki, and Micmac; a complete liturgical calendar; and short descriptions of the most important missions.

2008 • 160pp • hardback • 978-1-889758-89-3 • $44.95

Available from Evolution Publishing
www.evolpub.com

CPSIA information can be obtained
at www.ICGtesting.com
Printed in the USA
VHW031025011121
20260BV00004B/71